A Moose, Monsters & Melville

A Moose, Monsters & Melville

A Journey to the Far Beyond

WRITTEN BY:
PATRICIA H. WILLIAMS

ILLUSTRATED BY:
JAYNE ALLISON

**A Moose, Monsters and Melville
A Journey to the Far Beyond**

Copyright 2024 Patricia H. Williams

All rights reserved. No part of this publication or the characters within it may be reproduced, distributed, or transmitted in any form or by any means including photocopying, recording, or other electronic or mechanical methods without prior permission of the publisher. For permission, contact: pat@expansivejourney.com. Neither the author nor the publisher assumes any responsibility or liability whatsoever on behalf of the consumer or reader of this material nor can be held responsible for the use of the information provided in this book.

Illustrations by Jayne Allison

Editing by Christopher J. Williams

ISBN: 979-8-89109-992-0 - paperback
ISBN: 979-8-89109-993-7 - ebook
ISBN: 979-8-89109-969-2 - hardcover

First edition 2024

Visit: www.expansivejourney.com

To my remarkable sons, Christopher and Nicholas and the *Expansive Journey* we have shared.

Acknowledgments

One of the most important things I learned in my own journey to the Far Beyond in authoring this book – which has been in my heart for over a decade – is it has come to fruition only because I had the love, support and encouragement of so many people.

It gives me incredible pleasure to be able to say thank you to those who have played a significant role in its birth.

Although both long ago passed away to a new form of expression my parents, Claude and Ethel Rudy, gave me a love of reading, an appreciation of "words" and their power. One of my fondest memories is being curled up in a comfy chair in our living room, reading.

My sons, Chris and Nick both played a substantial role in the creation of the book. Chris used his professional editing skills as the editor of the book. Nick developed the website (www.

expansivejourney.com) and provides continual technology support. Both have talked me off the ledge a number of times. You both light up my life!

To Jayne Allison for her amazing illustrations that made Moose and all his supporting characters come to life on the page. Your talent is off the charts!

Nancy Barlow, a dear friend and my publicist, your expertise in orchestrating the launch with ease, grace and success is invaluable. KC Keefer, a photographer extraordinaire has demonstrated patience with me beyond reason. Brittany Plumeri, my publishing coach, has been supportive throughout this journey.

So many good friends have been willing to listen to my ups and my downs as I often made the journey more complicated and challenging than it needed to be. Sally Wurr, a best-selling author in her own right, and a good friend for decades has been so helpful and available to keep me on task and to answer even the most obvious questions that I continued to pose.

And there are my "Girlz!" Thank you, Theresa Colantuono, Sonja Lindeman, Janice Lohman and Candy Stephens. You all kept me standing in Spiritual Principle and remembering for me when I was unable to that all is well. And you were always ready to listen to me and bring me back to reason!

And my "Tribe!" This group of women have been with me longer than Moosey and have been a part of this journey in ways that I cannot list in this small space. Lori DuBois, Marilyn Harmacek, Darcy Pace and Judy Stokes – I cannot imagine this journey without you. You have always had faith even when mine wavered.

And so many others that have been a part of the journey, listening to my never-ending talk of Moose, a critter named Melville and the monsters they meet along the way. Thank you, my special mother-step, Mary Rudy and her daughter Elizabeth Bigham; Kathy Reis; Jean Bogar; Vel Frahm; Carol Buxton; Brian Schuett; Steve and Jody Troop whom I have known since we were growing up together in Alamogordo, New Mexico. And finally to all of my neighbors who have listened to my enthusiastic chatter now for several years.

Life in the Village

Once upon a time in a land not so far away lived Melville. Melville was – well truthfully, it was not particularly clear what Melville was. There was no doubt however that he was adorable. What made him even more special was that he never thought of himself as any better than the others in his Village. His Village was important to him.

Melville loved his daily routine. He always prepared a breakfast of frosted flakes and berries; he played with his zoozat (rather like a cat) and took pride in being organized and in control.

Melville loved watching the Village monkeys. It was his contribution to his Village. He especially liked the babies. Melville could talk to the baby monkeys – **no one else could do that!**

Sometimes Melville was sad because he rarely had time to climb the trees that surrounded his community and to look out toward the Far Beyond. He LOVED the times he could spend climbing the trees and thinking of the Far Beyond, but again today it was too dark by the time he was able to "get to it!"

However, Melville always made time to visit with Moose! Moose always made Melville feel good; he asked Moose important questions. Moose gave him advice which truthfully, Melville did not always take. However, **Melville knew Moosey was wise**.

Today as Melville began his time with Moose, for the 856th time the big creature encouraged Melville to take a journey of his own. "Instead of climbing the trees to view the Far Beyond, take your own journey. I KNOW you are ready!" Moosey's voice was soft and raspy like his head which Melville loved to sit on while they had these important conversations – even though he had to move around his antlers! Despite Moosey's height, Melville felt safe, snuggled into his shoulders, holding on to his antlers if needed for balance. He was not, however, excited to have another conversation about taking this journey.

Melville had every excuse ever invented in his land and probably many others, close and far away, as to why he should NOT embark upon this journey. "KAPOOCHEE!" he said over and over. "KAPOOCHEE! KAPOOCHEE!" There is no translation, but his resistance was obvious.

More than a little exasperated, Melville spouted the reasons why this journey was impossible: "Who would take care of my zoozat? My hovel cannot be left empty! My sister would never get along without me. No one else can TALK to **my** baby monkeys! But Moosey, mostly, mostly I am so AFRAID of the MONSTERS that live on the path to the Far Beyond!"

KAPOOCHEE!

Moose gazed at Melville with such complete love and acceptance that Melville had no choice but to take several deep breaths and feel better.

"**You can do this**," said that soft and raspy voice. Open to the possibilities. Think about the journey and think about the Far Beyond. Remember how you love the trees. Imagine touching the trees, sitting under a tree, and taking a nap. Moosey knew how much Melville **LOVED** to nap.

"Go home now, consider what I have said, get a good night's sleep and see what tomorrow brings! And remember that the Great Spirit is always with you!"

While Melville was still apprehensive about this journey, he did trust Moose with all his heart and soul. As he walked back to his hovel, he began to wonder if in fact, this journey was possible. "Moosey would never let anything happen to me," he thought. So, he did what the wise Moose suggested and went to sleep thinking about all those things Moose recommended. And if truth be told, he had wonderful dreams about the possibilities in the journey toward the Far Beyond!

The tomorrow dawned as was to be expected, and Melville woke up early from a dream about the journey. In spite of a vague remembrance of cliffs, waterfalls and even a monster or two, he had a clear sense of anticipation! He wondered what could happen this day that would enable him to go on this incredible journey? As he started to think especially about Madula, monkeys, and monsters he began to feel both sad and scared. However, as he remembered Moosey's faith and his belief in the Great Spirit, he thought instead of the beauty and adventure he **just knew** existed on the way to the Far Beyond!

Melville took some comfort in his morning routine even though this day did not seem like any other that he could remember. He talked aloud to his zoozat which helped him get his thoughts to settle down a bit. He made an even bigger bowl than usual of his frosted flakes and berries. Somehow, he felt a little better. However, he knew that he had to decide about visiting the Far Beyond with Moosey and it weighed heavily on his mind.

It seemed like no matter which decision he made about this journey someone would be unhappy. "How can I choose?" he said aloud to the zoozat who ignored him and continued with its own breakfast.

Just before Melville was ready to leave to watch the monkeys, he heard a hard knock at his hovel door. "Who could be visiting so early?" he wondered. He opened the door to find his sister, Madula. As she burst through the open door, she began sobbing uncontrollably. Of course, Melville was concerned and tried to calm her down. He said, "Madula, Madula take a breath!" as he led her to a chair on which to sit down. That did not seem to help as she continued to hold her head and sob.

He quickly went to the kitchen and poured her a cup of warm snoodle (a drink a little like milk but much sweeter). "Here, drink this!" And finally, she was able to take a breath and a small sip of the drink.

Although she still had tears falling, she began to tell Melville what happened. "On my block all the hovels are damaged. There was a big water line break under our pathway and water flowed everywhere!" Just saying it caused her to start crying a bit harder. "Now, now," said Melville, "you are here now, you are OK, just finish your story." She explained that the inside of her hovel was not significantly damaged as the water had stayed mostly in the street. "However, Melville, we cannot stay in our hovels while all the repairs are made under the pathways. And that could take at least a month!"

Melville was as horrified as Madula, but suddenly realized that he was going to be late to his responsibility to tend the Monkeys! "Oh, my! Do not worry! Stay here today. We will sort this out when I return."

Melville raced to the monkey habitat because he was so late! It was hard for him not to imagine all sorts of terrible things happening to "his" monkeys. As he got closer, he suddenly thought about what Moose would have said if he was here. ***"Remember not to imagine all the bad things that can happen - think about the good things instead!"*** So, Melville began to think of the Monkeys all safe-and-sound with his helper, Benny, a young one from the Village. It will not matter that he cannot talk to them as long as they are safe!

As he rounded the corner and quietly approached the babies, he saw immediately that they were safe. He was so happy! However, he did not say anything immediately to Benny. As he stood in the shadows at the edge of the Habitat what he heard was astonishing!

His helper, Benny, such a young one, was TALKING – Yes, TALKING – to the babies! "How can this be," thought Melville? It was hard for him to believe that this could be happening, much less understand it. Melville had spent many years feeling as though watching after the monkeys and especially talking to them made him special and most valuable to his Village and community. What was he to do now?

Before he could decide what he should do, the young one turned around and saw Melville. He had a look of horror on his face. "You can talk to those babies?' asked Melville. "Yes, sire," he said, "I never told anyone because I thought you would be angry. Please do not make me leave – I love the monkeys!" It was clear to Melville that indeed, Benny loved the baby monkeys. And as happy as they seemed to see Melville, it was also obvious that the babies loved Benny too. He realized he was not truly angry with Benny – just surprised and a little unsettled about the entire situation.

Suddenly, Melville thought about the adventure with Moosey he was considering. As he thought a little longer, he knew that his **Kapoochees** – except possibly the monsters – had evaporated! He assured Benny that all was well – it could not hurt to have two watchers of the Monkeys – and especially two that could talk to the babies.

At the end of the day after the monkeys were settled in for the upcoming night, Melville and Benny walked away together. Melville knew that he needed to reassure Benny that he was not angry. Melville also knew that sometimes the unexpected offers many gifts that are in themselves unexpected. He made sure that Benny knew that he was not mad and that he was happy – especially for the Monkeys – that there was another that could talk to them. "There is much going on at this moment that I must settle," continued Melville. "Plan to watch and talk to the Monkeys tomorrow and you and I will chat then. Please do not worry – all is well!"

To be honest, Melville was a bit exhausted after the crazy day. And it was not over yet! He had to go home, work with Madula to figure out her problems, and he knew that Moose was waiting for his decision about the journey. It seemed too much to take care of, especially at the moment! And then he remembered what Moose would say to him when he felt overwhelmed or unsure of what to do next. Moose would say, "Ask the Great Spirit what is the right path, the answer to the question and to guide and direct you to the right choice!" He realized that it would be best to take some time and do that right now, no matter if it caused him to get home a little later.

And so that is what Melville did!

By the time Melville arrived at his hovel, he felt calm and reasonably sure that he and Madula could solve her immediate problem. And that they did! He went with her to her hovel as the Village was allowing the residents to go inside one more time to gather anything that they needed while they were away. It was helpful that Madula did not have any pets – she loved Melville's zoozat and was looking forward to spending time with it while she stayed with Melville.

It was going to be a little crowded in Melville's hovel with the addition of Madula. It was truly designed for one person (and maybe a zoozat). Melville gave Madula his small bedroom and agreed to sleep on the sofa although he knew it was not particularly comfortable. He also knew that it was the right thing to do while they worked out a plan.

Needless to say, both Melville and Madula were exhausted after this extraordinary day and decided to have a quick supper of leftovers from Melville's meal the day before and settle in for the night.

Honestly, Melville did not sleep particularly well. The excitement of the day – the uncomfortable sofa – some pressure about the journey – all kept him from a sound sleep. When the zoozat woke him up because it was hungry, at first Melville could not believe it was morning. As he sat up, however, he realized that he felt amazing. There was a sense of peace and calm that had settled over him and he absolutely knew that he would make his decision this day about the **_Journey to the Far Beyond_** and that whatever the decision, it would be the correct one.

He quickly checked on Benny and the monkeys, but he knew that after that it was time to talk to Moose.

He found Moose in one of his favorite places munching a bush. "I am ready!" said Melville. "You **KNEW** Moosey, you knew that I would go!"

"So did you," said that wise Moose! "So did you!" "Moosey, what about the monsters?" Melville was still somewhat concerned about this adventure. In his soft, somewhat scratchy voice, Moose said "Melville, the monsters live mostly in your imagination! Just know that and let those monsters go and all will be well."

"I could do it, Moosey, if you would be with me. I don't know if I can do this without you."

Again, Moosey, looked at Melville with so much love and said, "Melville, of course, I am going with you. Have you not understood – **I AM YOUR GUIDE, YOUR FRIEND, YOUR PARTNER ALWAYS!**

Last Minute Butterflies

While it all sounded so logical last week while Melville was busy preparing for the journey and talking often to Moosey, the day before the big adventure was to begin, Melville suddenly stood still in the monkey habitat and tears began to fill his eyes. "How can I be away from my monkeys? How much will my babies grow while I am gone?"

Even though all the preparations had been made, it unexpectedly seemed easier to tell Moose that he could not go than to take that leap and leave his monkeys, his Village and all that was so familiar. Telling Moose he had changed his mind would **not** be easy, however, once it was done he could go back to his monkeys and the daily routine that made him comfortable and happy.

Benny returned from tending to a couple of the older monkeys that were clearly having some problems getting along. He could tell immediately that his friend and teacher was sad. He put his arm around Melville and asked him what was wrong.

"I am not sure I want to go on this adventure," admitted Melville, trying to stop the tears from flowing. "I will miss the monkeys too much. I am afraid that they will forget me. I am not sure Madula can live at my hovel without me and take good care of my zoozat. And mostly, Benny, I AM AFRAID OF THE MONSTERS THAT I KNOW LIVE ON THE WAY TO THE FAR BEYOND!"

KAPOOCHEE!

Benny decided quickly to be truthful and say what seemed obvious to him. "Melville, take a breath, stop being a silly goose and remember that these are the same excuses you had before. You know that they have already been taken care of and Madula will be fine. I will check on her often. The monkeys – old and young – will be safe. Do you not trust me? YOU NEED TO GO TALK TO MOOSEY – SOON!"

It took quite a while for Melville to find Moose. He almost gave up when there he was! The big creature was enjoying an early dinner, munching on a mixture of twigs, bark, leaves, and delighting in a scruffy shrub. It took a lot of food to keep Moosey full and happy! Moose looked up and noticed Melville and could immediately tell that Melville was troubled. One of Moose's best qualities was his ability to see when another was unhappy.

"What is wrong, Melville? I am so excited to leave tomorrow for our adventure. Are you ready?" Melville had held his tears in for too long and they began to flow. He was so conflicted – to go or not to go? "I am too scared to go on this journey, Moose. I am sorry but I am not big and brave like you **and** besides, I will miss the monkeys, Madula and my zoozat too much!"

You would think that Moose would be tired of Melville's excuses and finally decide to head in the direction of the Far Beyond without Melville.

But the wise and loving Moose did no such thing. As before, he looked at Melville with much love and said, "Oh, yes you can! I will be with you and again, the monsters that you are imagining in your head are far worse than anything we might meet on our wonderful adventure. They talked for a bit. Then Moose said, "Go home – get ready – relax and snuggle in and get a good night's sleep and I will see you early tomorrow, just after the sunrise right here." With a look at Melville of pure love and affection, Moose went back to dinner!

Although he was still a bit troubled about what would come in the morning, when he got home Melville began to pack up the few things he could fit in his pack to take on the journey. It was hard to choose but Madula helped him – keeping him from packing too much! What he really wanted was to take Madula and the zoozat with him. He knew in his heart, however, that this was his journey – not theirs – and he had to do this on his own with Moosey.

He slept better than he expected and there were some dreams that he only barely remembered. He awoke refreshed and feeling more ready for the Far Beyond than he had ever been. The pesky butterflies in his tummy were gone. After a quick breakfast, a hug for Madula and a pet for the zoozat, he grabbed his pack and was off to the place he and Moosey had agreed to meet.

Once there, he saw the wonderful fuzzy Moose, climbed up on his back, settled into the special place on his head, holding on to his antlers for balance. He was excited and ready!

Together, Moosey and Melville began an adventure that they would remember forever and always!

The Journey

The day was beautiful, excellent for the beginning of a special journey. Although the sun was still low in the sky, it was already warming up and it was sure to be a wonderful start to the voyage.

As they rounded the first bend on their path toward what Moose whispered was the direction of the Far Beyond, they found themselves in a beautiful place with tall green trees on one side and a narrow bubbling stream on the other. It made Melville want to stop and enjoy the beauty. And if truth be told, it put off the inevitable trek to the Far Beyond where he was still convinced many monsters lived. KAPOOCHE!

Moosey would have none of that, however, and just kept walking along the path! And since he did not stop, Melville had no choice but to stay snuggled into his spot on the top of Moose's head and accept that they were, in fact, heading toward the Far Beyond. They followed the stream for almost an hour and it the trees were bigger and closer together. It was beautiful but a little bit scary to Melville. He was also getting a little cramped on Moosey's head and was hoping they would stop soon. But even as he had that thought, he was afraid that if they stopped maybe the monsters would indeed appear.

Just then, they came around a curve and there was a clearing in the woods. Moose stopped and said to Melville, "I think this is an excellent place to stop and get some water and a little snack." Melville was grateful for that suggestion even though he was still a little uneasy about the monsters. He even said to Moose, "But Moosey what about the monsters that I KNOW live here!" Moose actually snorted! He was getting a little tired of Melville's constant worry about the monsters that he knew were not anything to be concerned about. "Melville," he said, "First, I am telling you again that there are no monsters of which to be afraid on the journey. Second, if you are still afraid, ask the Great Spirit to guide us and keep us safe." Even though he was a little irritated with

Melville – partly because Moose, too, was ready for a break and some food – he understood that Melville was truly afraid and wanted to make him feel as safe as Moose knew he was.

Although there was no question he was a bit scared as he scrambled off Moose's back, Melville was also hungry and thirsty! He got right into his pack and pulled out some of the food that he brought. Yum! Moose immediately found a fat bush and started munching on the leaves. The stream provided water for them both. It was a nice break and even Melville began to feel comfortable as they finished their lunch.

Melville did have a question for Moose, however. "Moosey, what are we going to do when we get to the Far Beyond? Moose took a little bit of time to answer, but then said, "It is not what we are going to do there, my little friend, it is what we will feel when we are there. It is a sacred place – filled with the Great Spirit – and we will feel that presence and know that all is well. What I want for you is for you to be able to take that feeling home with you. It will make your life magical if you do!"

This was a lot for Melville to understand but he was willing to trust Moosey and to try to get what was being said. And he thought it would be a good thing if the Great Spirit could keep the monsters away!

Soon it was time for the two adventurers to be on their way again. Melville climbed up on Moose, settled in and off they went again. Although Melville thought he saw a monster peek out between the trees, he was determined to trust both Moose and the Great Spirit as they took off again toward the Far Beyond.

As they continued on their trek, the forest became thick and the path narrower. It made Melville happy that he had settled into Moose's head and could hang on to his antlers for balance and did not have to be walking in the thick forest. Moose knew that his friend was still quite afraid as they continued the journey, but this wise animal also knew that it was good for him to be trying something new and that he would at some point realize that the journey was fun.

The sun was low in the sky when Moose said, "OK, we need to find a place to settle in for the night before it is completely dark." Melville had not thought of spending the night in the forest. He thought that they would get to the Far Beyond before nightfall. "Kapooche," he said to himself not wanting Moosey to know how scared he really was.

Moose found the perfect spot – off the path and surrounded by lots of small bushes and trees for shelter – and immediately began to devour another bush or two for his dinner. Melville pulled out his food from his little pack and was happy that he had brought more tasty items. Moose also showed him that many of the bushes around them had fat berries on them which was a good addition to Melville's dinner.

Both Moosey and Melville were tired after their long trek. Moosey liked that the spot had good coverage – hidden from any bears that might be around. Bears were one of the few animals that Moosey had to be concerned about!

The big moose laid down up against some of the brush to settle in for the night. Melville looked around – still thinking about the monsters – and quickly snuggled up beside Moosey and immediately felt safe. Looking at Melville with much love, Moosey began to quietly sing a song about the Great Spirit to Melville. "**Oh, gentle Spirit, peace and sleep to bring, waking us in the morning with love and joy about which to sing**!"

Needless to say, Melville almost immediately fell asleep safe in the presence of his precious Moosey and the Great Spirit.

The morning dawned early and beautiful. Even with the shade from the trees, the warmth of the sun could already be felt. Moosey, of course, woke up very hungry. He nudged Melville to wake him up before he got up on his long four legs. Melville was dreaming about his monkeys – a much better dream than about the monsters. That made Melville happy as he got up and stretched. He was already looking forward to more berries for breakfast. Moosey immediately began chomping down on another bush.

Soon they were on their way again. They walked in silence for the first hour. Both were lost in their own thoughts and enjoying the beauty of the day. Melville broke the silence and asked Moosey, "How much longer will it take us to get to the Far Beyond?" As usual, the great Moose looked at Melville with much love and replied, "We are not in a rush so we will stop a couple of times on our way. There is a wonderful place

I want to show you. And of course, we will need to have some lunch!" That big Moose was hungry most of the time.

The rest of the morning was spent on an easy walk down the path toward the Far Beyond. There were birds singing beautiful songs, chipmunks and squirrels darting around hoping for some food, and they even spotted a beautiful deer in the distance. As the morning passed, it became warmer and sunnier. It was amazing. Melville lost his impatience and began to simply enjoy the journey. About the time Melville was hoping for a little break and to be able to get down from his spot on the top of Moosey's head, Moose stopped and said, "We have arrived at the wonderful spot I want you to see!" Melville scrambled down excited to see what Moose was going to show him.

As he followed Moose into the woods just a bit, there it was! Wow! It was the most wonderful waterfall he had ever seen – not that Melville had seen many waterfalls.

There was no doubt that it was amazing. Moosey and Melville stood together – one so big and the other so little – both enjoying the beautiful sight. They had much gratitude for the beauty. As they stood there, Melville looked on the

other side of Moosey and was shocked to see what looked like one of the monsters he had imagined lived in the Far Beyond. Instead of shouting at Moose, however, he took a minute and realized that this little creature was enjoying the view as much as he and Moosey were. And when he looked again, there was another and another – all simply looking at the beautiful waterfall. Moose glanced down at Melville and said, "See, Melville, the fear of these cute little guys was all made up in your head! While it is important to be aware of danger, it is also important not to imagine it when it is not there. Imagine all the good things – expect them – and be grateful for them. Just like this journey we are taking together. Let your joy spill over just like the waterfall we are seeing."

After a quick lunch, Moosey was ready to continue their journey. So all of them including the not very scary monsters pushed on toward the Far Beyond. Shortly, they came to a place that overlooked a beautiful valley. There was a path down the mountain heading toward the valley. Moose said, "We have arrived! We have reached the edge of the Far Beyond."

Melville looked at the path and knew that this part of his journey was complete. He was proud of himself, knew that he had learned much and had spent wonderful time with his beloved Moosey. As Moosey had said in the beginning, it was so much better to have taken the journey to the edge of the Far Beyond than to simply climb the trees in the village thinking about it. But as he said to Moosey in gratitude, "Mostly, mostly, Moosey, I learned that the Great Spirit is always with me and that while sometimes there can be real danger, the fear of my monsters was created in my head!"

BIOGRAPHIES

Patricia H. Williams has been writing since childhood. Writing assignments in elementary school were considered with enthusiasm. An essay earned her scholarship money for university. While her roommates would groan at the required writing, she loved it! And once in the business world, she was able to find opportunities to contribute via writing. The owner of two businesses over the years, writing was an integral part of both. She created stories – one about Dinky the Dinosaur - to entertain her young sons on the drive to pre-school. Writing a book was the next logical step. The vision of Moosey and sharing his message with children has been a dream for a decade.

Jayne Allison is a freelance artist and illustrator living in Brooklyn, New York. She works in oil paint, watercolor, ink, and mixed media, and is always looking to expand her repertoire by experimenting in different mediums. She draws inspiration from the children's book illustrators who influenced her childhood: Beatrix Potter, Ernest Shepard, and Sven Nordqvist, to name just a few! She also derives creativity from the whimsy that is present in the natural world. Jayne is also the illustrator for *Hocus-Porpoise* by Brenda Topping.

www.ingramcontent.com/pod-product-compliance
Lightning Source LLC
Chambersburg PA
CBHW061358010526
44107CB00012B/977